HITLER
ON TRIAL

Alan Cranston,
Mein Kampf, and
The Court of
World Opinion

Lorraine H. Tong

Hitler on Trial
Alan Cranston, *Mein Kampf,* and the Court of World Opinion

Stanford University granted permission for use of the photograph on the book cover of Alan M. Cranston. It was taken upon his graduation from Stanford in 1936.

Special discounts for bulk purchases of the paperback book are possible by contacting info@LHTproductions.com.

Cover design by Heidi Sutherlin; www.mycreativepursuits.com

ISBN # 978-0-9993889-1-4
Library of Congress Control Number: 2017915026

To Alan Cranston
Leader. Humanitarian. Peacemaker.

To My Grandfather Wu Ping–Yi
(Secretary to Sun Yat–sen)
who inspired me to love
China, America, and democracy

and

To all who love liberty and
fight evil, tyranny, and injustice in all forms

Acknowledgements

Writing a book is primarily a solitary undertaking, but its completion would not have been possible without the collective support of family, friends, and colleagues. Their friendship is a gift beyond measure. I am truly at a loss for words that would adequately express my heartfelt gratitude to so many, including:

Kai and Lauren for their enduring love and support,

Emily and James Thurber for their grace, wisdom, and friendship,

Dr. Rikki Baum for her insight, and keeping me on track while urging me to slow down.

Alan's sister Ruth Eleanor "R.E." Fowle, whom I first met on December 26, 1977, at her Los Altos home. Kim and Colette Cranston for their support and generosity in sharing their father with me after all these years. Special thanks to Alan's granddaughter Evan who took the photo of her father holding Alan's edition of *Mein Kampf.* They had an especially close connection.

I also express my deep appreciation to Matthew Wasniewski, Mary Rouvelas, Zoe Davis, Leigh

Chronister, as well as former Cranston staff, and colleagues in the Senate, House, and the Library of Congress.

Special thanks to:

The Library of Congress

Stanford University

Bancroft Library at University of California, Berkeley

U.S. District Court for the
Southern District of New York

National Archives

United States Holocaust Memorial Museum

Charles E. Beatley Central Library, Alexandria, Virginia

and

George F. Thuronyi, Editor

David Rice, Photographer

Before the Internet,
*there was **Alan Cranston**.*

Author's Note

Alan MacGregor Cranston served in the U.S. Senate for 24 years as Senator from California (1969–1993), 14 of which he served as Democratic Whip. I had the privilege of working as his legislative aide and advisor on foreign policy for eight of those years. He was also a candidate for President. On the rare occasions when we had a difference of opinion, I rationalized to myself, "Well, there was that Hitler thing."

The "Hitler thing" is the focus and purpose of this short book about Alan Cranston who exposed the full measure of Adolf Hitler's ideology and plans as set forth in *Mein Kampf (My Struggle)*. It recounts Cranston's own urgent *kampf* to alert the American public and the world about the danger that Hitler posed.

The scope of this book is a modest one. It does not pretend to be a comprehensive history of World War I, World War II, Hitler, Alan Cranston, or copyright law. It does not detail efforts by others to publish *Mein Kampf* in the United States. It does seek to give insight to the people and events that shaped young Alan into a 24–year old journalist who took on the threat of Hitler with both conviction and courage. It is about a seminal episode that set Cranston on a path of public service for the rest of his life as a man of peace, a man who strived to prevent war, and a man who fought for a just world that must be preserved for future generations.

Alan Cranston's own philosophy and definition of a leader reflected the teaching of Chinese philosopher Lao Tzu. I personally witnessed his consistent application of Lao Tzu's ideal of a good leader. He kept in his wallet this quote for half a century:

> *A leader is best*
> *When people barely know*
> *That he exists,*
> *Less good when*
>
> *They obey and acclaim him,*
> *Worse when*
>
> *They fear and despise him.*
> *Fail to honor people*
>
> *And they fail to honor you.*
> *But of a good leader,*
>
> *When his work is done,*
> *His aim fulfilled,*
> *They will all say,*
>
> *"We did this ourselves."*

Lao Tzu, c. 604–c. 531 B.C.

To this day, Alan Cranston's legacy resonates in the countless lives that he touched throughout his life in public service, inside and outside of government.

Edmund Burke said:

"The only thing necessary for the triumph of evil is for good men to do nothing."

Alan Cranston did something.

Lorraine H. Tong
October 2017

"Intensity, big plans, no little plans, that was the Alan Cranston that I knew. Most of us would consider it a successful career if we did nothing other than be sued by Adolf Hitler. But here's a fellow, a young man who came back from Europe as a correspondent, who felt obliged to translate accurately "Mein Kampf," who felt obliged to begin a crusade to expose Adolf Hitler."

Vice President Joseph R. Biden,
Then–Senator Biden, led the Senate delegation to Alan
Cranston's Memorial. Excerpt from Remarks at the
Memorial Celebration for Alan MacGregor Cranston
Grace Cathedral, San Francisco, CA, January 16, 2001
Memorial Tributes and Addresses (Reprinted in the
Congressional Record, February 8, 2001)

Contents

Introduction

Alan MacGregor Cranston was born on June 19, 1914, in Palo Alto, California. Nearly 6,000 miles away during that year, 25–year old Adolf Hitler volunteered and began service in the 16th Bavarian Reserve Infantry Regiment of the German army. That same year, a series of events plunged Europe into war. Devastating in its destructive carnage that spanned the earth, the war was known as the Great War. Later, it was designated a number: World War I.

Cranston and Hitler could not have been more different. Their upbringing, temperament, values, and ideology were a study in stark contrasts, yet their lives were destined to intersect.

By 1933, Hitler had become Chancellor of Germany and orchestrated the rise of the Third Reich. By 1939, Hitler had already been executing his plans as laid out in his manifesto *Mein Kampf* for several years. Cranston used Hitler's own words in *Mein Kampf* – which had been sanitized in the American–published version – to expose his true intent for the world. He translated and wrote a condensed unexpurgated version of Hitler's racist manifesto that laid out his Aryan supremacy ideology, his strategy for world domination, and chilling anti–Semitism. Hitler's American publisher, Houghton Mifflin Company, sued Noram Publishing Company, publisher of the Cranston edition, for copyright infringement in a U.S. district court.

Five months after the Cranston version of *Mein Kampf* hit the newsstands, Hitler invaded Poland. This military action followed a chain of increasingly aggressive events that led to the outbreak of war in Europe and subsequently to World War II. Cranston, a man born when WWI began, acted decisively to alert the world to Hitler, monster and master planner of what history would record as WWII, including the horrific genocide of six million Jews. Various sources estimate total military and civilian casualties on six continents ranged from a staggering 60 to 80 million.

.

Part I

Young Alan Cranston

Alan MacGregor Cranston, born in Palo Alto, California on June 19, 1914, was welcomed into the world with love and joyful anticipation. His parents, William and Carol Cranston, had lost their first son to illness seven years earlier. His older sister by five years, Ruth Eleanor, known to her friends as R.E., became her little brother's companion and champion throughout his life. Although his father's real estate company had been successful, the Cranston family experienced serious financial losses caused by the 1906 San Francisco earthquake and subsequently, like millions of other Americans, struggled through the Great Depression.

On the whole, young Alan Cranston enjoyed an active, happy, and comfortable childhood. William Cranston's fortunes improved and the family moved to a home on a farm with acres of velvet green meadows with a pond. The expanse of land and wide pristine vistas gave Alan a place to roam free as well as a serene setting for quiet thoughts, reflection, and dreams of the future. He flourished under the California sun and later became a true California son and a champion of the environment. His love of and connection with nature were the foundation for his strong determination to preserve the land in California and the nation to remain unspoiled for generations to come.

It was the ideal place for a boy of his boundless energy where he ran, rode horses and bikes, and played football and other sports with his equally energetic friends. According to his sister, the boys hatched all kinds of adventures and pranks like other normal boys of that age. This was where his imagination took flight. The constancy of a nurturing family provided a solid base that shaped his character. Decades later, Cranston attributed his initiative and self-reliance to his parents' guidance and wisdom in allowing him to make decisions early in life. His upbringing gave him the confidence to leave his safe and unspoiled home, Villa

Warec (named by his father for the initials William, Alan, Ruth Eleanor, and Carol), to strike out on his own. He ventured overseas and realized his dreams of being a foreign correspondent, and overcame obstacles to achieve success.

Having lost a son before Alan, it must not have been easy for William and Carol to give Alan such latitude and later to accept his decision to travel so far from home. On his part, Alan appreciated his parents. His frequent letters to them and his sister from his travels reflected a sensitive and thoughtful nature.

For the times, Alan was well traveled at an early age. When he was 12, overseas travel began in 1926 with his parents and R.E. In 1926, 1928, and 1930, the Cranston family visited England, France, Germany, Czechoslovakia, Holland, Belgium, Norway, and Sweden. Then, in the summer of 1934, Alan visited France, Austria, Hungary, and Germany as an unpaid correspondent for the Mountain View *Register-Leader*, and covered the trial of those who assassinated Austrian Chancellor Engelbert Dollfuss in Vienna. In August that summer, after the death of President Hindenburg, Hitler consolidated his power by merging the two positions of president and chancellor into one and declared himself Fuhrer of a new German Reich – – the Third Reich.

Slender in his youth, Alan developed a wiry and athletic build by his mid–teens and finally reached 6' 2" in height. His large, dark brown eyes often had an intense focus but his freckled face would crinkle up with easy humor that he inherited from his parents. According to R.E., Alan's joyful optimism came from their father and his cool judgment from their mother. He was drawn to the written word early on, and his talent and diligence were rewarded. At Mountain View High School, he was elected president of the Boys' League (the boys' student body) and showed wit in the school newspaper's column, *School Daze*. The column appeared regularly in the *Mountain Eagle*, which was reprinted in the local paper, Mountain View's *Register–Leader*.

While the fledgling reporter liked writing stories about other people and events, he was private about his own life. In her book, R.E. described Alan's dedication to writing his unfiltered thoughts in diaries, which he kept for some years beginning in his late teens. The front page of one diary bore this warning:

"KEEP OUT! Yes, You."[1]

A voracious reader, his tastes ran the gamut. Among the authors he read and admired were Mark Twain, Charles Dickens, and Shakespeare. *Treasure Island* was a boyhood favorite. In college, he particularly loved reading about Leonardo da Vinci. As he got older, he read biographies of Lincoln and other presidents, senators, and governors.

Cranston's resolve and sense of adventure may have been stamped in his DNA. He likely inherited the wanderlust and pioneer spirit from his Scottish ancestors on both sides of the family. All four grandparents moved to California in the 1800s. Politics was in his genes as well. His great–grandfather, Hiram Harlow Dixon, was a Vermont state senator. A grand uncle on his father's side, James Bolton from the Shetland Isles, served in the British House of Commons.[2]

The Cranstons enjoyed a wide circle of friends, many from the literary and journalistic world. They

---

[1] Eleanor Fowle, *Cranston, Senator from California*, Jeffrey Tarcher, Inc., Los Angeles, CA, 1984, p.10. Hereafter known as Fowle.,

[2] Fowle, p. 7.

were colorful, well–read, and well–traveled individuals who were open and vocal about their views on life and politics. A shy lot, they were not. Alan was very much a product of the free spirit and character that is intrinsically California, a young state of a young country. When Alan was born, California had been a state for only 64 years. William Cranston was a Republican, but politics did not affect his friendships and in fact, made for fascinating conversations that surrounded Alan. This was the world that influenced and began shaping young Alan, particularly William's best friend Fremont Older, a well–respected, pioneer journalist for the *Call Bulletin* newspaper.

Regular Sunday lunches were held at Villa Warec and sometimes at the Older residence. Young Alan absorbed stories of history and current events, stories that sparked his curiosity and hunger for adventure. According to R.E., Alan revered Fremont Older as "a model for the kind of man he later sought to become."

Gatherings at both Villa Warec and at the Olders' nearby ranch in Saratoga saw a varied steady stream of people: writers, political figures, and a host of unexpected guests, including some former convicts the Olders were trying to help get back into society. Alan was exposed to this diverse group from different professions, circumstances, and socio—economic backgrounds.

The population of Palo Alto in 1920 was 5,900 with almost no diversity— predominantly white with some Japanese, a few Chinese and blacks. [3] The Cranston's gardener who tended the extensive grounds of Villa Warec was a Japanese—American named Tanaka, which may have had a small measure in influencing Alan's early interaction with different races and cultures. [4]

When Fremont Older died, Alan sadly noted that the Sundays the Cranston family had with him had ended. Alan was 18 years old and perhaps this event made him realize that even a journalistic giant like Older, a man he respected, was all too mortal. At 18, Alan had an idea of what he wanted in life. In his personal diary, he wrote, "I want to make a real dent in the world." [5]

_____

[3]According to the Palo Alto Historical Association, the U.S. Census for Palo Alto's population was 5,900 in 1920. There were some Japanese but only a few Chinese and blacks.

[4]Cranston later worked with First Lady Eleanor Roosevelt against the internment of Japanese—Americans during WWII.

[5]The title of Judith Robinson's two—volume biography is *Alan Cranston Senator from California—Making a Dent in the World,* Telegraph Hill Press, San Francisco, CA, 2008, and Fowle, p. 10.

The widow of Fremont Older, Cora, a writer and historian in her own right, introduced Alan to Milton K. "Pop" Smith, editor of the Mountain View *Register–Leader.* The introduction led to an opportunity to write a regular column for the local newspaper. Alan's euphoria is expressed in one of his diaries:

> *"I typed (an article on the 1932 Olympic Games in Los Angeles) and took it over to the Mountain View Register Leader office. "Pop" Smith barely glanced at it and said, "Yes. I'll be glad to take it." He told me to come around Friday, the day the paper comes out and he'll pay me then. I s'pose I'll get about a dollar for it. WHOOPEE!!! AT LAST I'VE SOLD SOMETHING! Am I happy."*[6]

A dollar was certainly a very respectable sum for a cub reporter. More importantly, he was published and that validated his talent and boosted his confidence to continue his quest to become a foreign correspondent.

Alan and the editor did not always hold the same views, and the relationship exposed him to views different from his own. Still, a good friendship

---

[6] Fowle, p.10.

emerged. Cranston's skill in being able to forge friendships with those holding divergent and even opposing views, became indispensable then and even more importantly when he later covered world events as a foreign correspondent and still later, as a Senator representing California. An effective Senator must often build coalitions with political rivals, negotiate, and bring disparate groups together to resolve differences and achieve legislative successes. Alan Cranston did reach across the political aisle to get things done. His leadership skills were recognized, as evidenced by the election of his colleagues to serve as the Democratic Whip for 14 of his 24 years in the United States Senate.

Three Passions

Alan met Geneva McMath on a blind date after his return from Europe in 1939. They married the following year and a few years later had two sons, Robin and Kim. When Robin was killed by speeding car, Alan experienced the devastating agony that only parents whose children predecease them can understand. In describing his father's main passions, other than the love of his family, Kim said Alan was inspired by three key motivators that shaped him. These three passions were track and field, adventure, and journalism. All three were evident throughout his life as confirmed by family and friends as well as those who worked with and for him.[7] They wove their influences throughout a life that eventually led to politics. They were the essence of an indomitable spirit that let few things or people stop him once he set his mind on a path or cause. He was also guided by twin practices: reflection and study of an issue from all angles and sides followed by analysis—characteristics of a solid journalist.

TRACK AND FIELD

Running came naturally to Alan and became an enduring passion from childhood to his 80s. As a sprinter, Alan enjoyed this lifetime sport from his carefree days running through the meadows at Villa Warec to success as a high school track star and then as a valued member of the nation's number one track–and–field relay team at Stanford University. Cranston's record: 9.9 seconds for the 100–yard dash, 48 seconds for the 440–yard dash. Although 48 seconds was significant, he did not make the cut for the Summer Olympics. He was close. It was a sobering

---

[7] The author met with Kim and Colette Cranston in November 2015 to discuss Alan's early years. and to visit Alan Cranston's personal library in their Los Altos, CA, home. The library was much the way Alan had left it when he died on December 31, 2000.

lesson. He examined the actions of others closely and his own no less so. After self–evaluation, he addressed this setback (and others he would encounter later in life) by looking forward and not backward with regrets. Practical and at times philosophical, Alan was a man who did not waste time wallowing in useless exercises and recriminations. He determined to do better. As a result, he developed greater discipline and focus in track. Cranston's self–discipline was to spill over into other parts of his life. He could and did focus like a laser beam when he set his mind to it. It was his "can do" mindset that helped him overcome obstacles and achieve his goals in various endeavors throughout his personal and professional life.

During a brief time at Stanford, his mind, however, was focused on a young woman, and he became distracted. Learning from that experience, he renewed his determination to concentrate on his goals. His determination and discipline were not limited to track. He applied them to achieve goals throughout his life. Decades later, he won the world's 100–yard record for over 55–year–old sprinters (18.6 seconds).[8] When he retired from the Senate to live in Los Altos, he returned

---

[8]Lloyd Shearer, "Alan Cranston—Fastest Man in the Senate," *Parade Magazine, The Washington Post*, Feb. 6, 1972, p.16.ed

to the familiar Stanford campus and its track where he had first made his mark as an integral and valued member of the university's celebrated field relay team.

ADVENTURE

Reading newspapers, tuning in to the radio, listening to his elders' conversations and then joining in their discussions contributed to his early education and development that would help shape his curiosity and thinking process. The world fascinated him, and he was in a big hurry to explore all the adventures it had to offer. Traveling brought new adventures, experience, and learning. He was fascinated by other peoples, languages, and cultures. He studied German, Spanish, Italian, and French. He began college at Pomona College in California (June 1932 – December 1933), and transferred to Stanford University in January1934 as a sophomore. and spent a summer at the University of Mexico immersed in Spanish language and culture.

Stanford was among American universities that joined an effort to foster better U.S.–German relations through the establishment of student exchange programs with German universities. Alan spent a semester in Germany in 1934. During that stay and his post–Stanford work as a foreign correspondent, he saw the power of the Nazi party's propaganda and the anti–Semitism.

His love of adventure beyond America's borders, and witnessing exciting but potentially dangerous events led his father to express concern to R.E. of potential disaster in the locations where Alan pursued stories and new experiences.

JOURNALISM

Young Alan's first ambition was to be a cartoonist.[9] He spent hours poring over comic strips, copying them, then progressed to drawing his own. Singing was also a source of enjoyment. Once, in mid–song, Alan suddenly forgot the words and found three pairs of eyes, those of his family, staring at him. Years later, he claimed to R.E. that this embarrassment "set back my public speaking about twenty years."[10] Alan had a creative streak and a talent for writing which was apparent early on. His love of the written word grew stronger, and he developed a knack for snappy and

---

[9]Cranston became life–long friends with Lee Falk, creator and author of King Features comic strips of *The Phantom* and Mandrake the Magician. They were co–playwriters for *The Big Story* about a foreign correspondent.

[10] Fowle, p. 6.

riveting leads. His innate instinct for cutting to the heart of a subject and sharp writing style engaged readers.

At Stanford, he also exercised a creative, bold streak in supporting a non–sorority candidate for queen. She had the distinctively memorable nickname "bedroom eyes," according to R.E. who followed and chronicled her brother's life. This time, Alan's writing took the unusual form of hiring a plane to skywrite Bedroom Eyes' real name as an attention–grabbing stunt that riveted all eyes on the Stanford campus skyward. The unorthodox campaign ad for a university race was hugely successful and raised a lot of money. However, it served to rally the opposition that supported a sorority candidate, and in turn, raised even more funds against Bedroom Eyes.

Bedroom Eyes lost the election.

His triple loves of running, adventure, and writing all converged seamlessly with his aspiration to be a foreign correspondent. Speed on the track and meeting press deadlines were similar–both had clear unambiguous end points and were inflexible. They, in fact, had common elements. One required physical agility and stamina, while the other demanded mental agility and ability to reach the goal. There was no going back to rerun a race nor to missed deadlines when editors and printing presses were waiting to put out the paper. If the facts in the article were wrong, a retraction would not only be embarrassing but reputations could be ruined. Cranston was able to master both of these seemingly divergent types of activities. Living his life as a foreign correspondent in covering and writing about exciting world events was Alan's idea of the ultimate adventure.

He wrote for *The Stanford Daily* while majoring in English, with a concentration on journalism and intensive study of German. After graduating in June 1936, he set out to fulfill his dream to become a foreign correspondent.

Young Alan with his older sister Ruth Eleanor, affectionately called R.E.
(From Cranston Family Collections)

Alan Cranston age 10,
(*From Cranston Family Collections*)

Alan Cranston in Race,
Stanford University Track Team
Courtesy of Global Security Institute

Alan Cranston, Graduation Photo
Stanford University Class of 1936

*We were discussing Germany. Mr. Older said,
"Hitler is a tyrant."*

*"Why is he a tyrant?" I asked to draw him out. "He is
doing what he thinks is right for Germany."*

*Mr. Older turned his big head, his whole body
towards me, and said, "Why—he kills people!"*

Alan Cranston
Diary entry, January 15, 1935 [11]

---

[11] Fowle, p. 13.

1924

Adolf Hitler writes *Mein Kampf.*

Part II

Adolf Hitler's *Mein Kampf*

In 1923, Adolf Hitler was arrested for his part in the unsuccessful attempt to overthrow the German government in what was known as the Beer Hall Putsch. Hitler was charged with and tried for treason. Found guilty and sentenced to five years, he served only nine months. The circumstances of his imprisonment were not typical and certainly not austere. Hitler served his sentence in Cell Number 7 in Germany's Landsberg prison.

It was during his imprisonment that he wrote his manifesto detailing his vision for Germany's expansion and world domination. Contrary to decades of what was accepted fact about his writing process, new research reveals that Hitler most likely did not dictate his manuscript to his trusted friend Rudolf Hess. Peter Ross Range, author of *1924: The Year That Made Hitler,* based on extensive research, reported that Hitler himself typed his book on an American–made Remington portable typewriter, a gift from a benefactor. According to Range's book, Hitler would read aloud his work in progress to Hess during his frequent visits throughout the months of Hitler's incarceration.[12] Hitler also had the luxury of time to reflect and to plot his return to power, using the book as the blueprint to invigorate and expand the Nazi party.

---

[12] The author met with Peter Ross Range to discuss his book, *1924: The Year that Made Hitler* (New York: Little, Brown and Company, 2016) on April 25, 2016.

Hitler's Foreword in *Mein Kampf*

On April 1, 1924, I commenced serving my sentence in the prison fortress of Landsberg on the Lech, according to decision rendered by the People's Court of Munich.

I was thus able to undertake a task frequently demanded of me, a task which, I, too, felt would be of service to the Movement. I decided to set down the story of our progress.

Also, I found opportunity to portray my own development – necessary if this book is to be understood and the filthy legends built up about me by the Jew press are to be destroyed. I address myself here not to strangers, but to followers of the Movement, strong–hearted followers who seek more intimate enlightenment.

I know that people are won more by the spoken than by the written word, that every great world movement depends upon great speakers, not upon great writers. But the principles of a doctrine must be laid down for eternity.

This, then, is a stone which I add to our common structure.

THE AUTHOR
Landsberg on the Lech
Prison Fortress

Hitler originally named his book, *Four and a Half Years of Struggle Against Lies, Stupidity and Cowardice*. He was disabused of his idea for this awkward, wordy, and possibly unmarketable book title by the manager of his publishing company. The ultimate result was the publication of *Mein Kampf* (English translation: *My Struggle* or *My Battle*). The manuscript was initially written in two volumes. The first volume, subtitled *Eine Albrechnung* (A Reckoning), was published in 1925; the second, subtitled *Die Nationalissozalistische Bewegung* (The Nazi Movement), in 1927. Thereafter, the two were combined into a single volume and its title shortened to *Mein Kampf*.

It is perverse irony that Hitler's punishment for his part to overthrow the government, the very government he sought to depose, essentially financed the creation of *Mein Kampf*, and laid the foundation for his subsequent triumphant return to rule the nation with unprecedented power. The government provided him with room and board in quarters that were luxurious compared to how one usually envisions a cell. Hitler's respectful and courteous behavior toward the prison's management was shrewd and accorded him many benefits. He was skillful, even gifted, in winning people over if he so chose. Only weeks after his imprisonment, he was permitted to celebrate his 35th birthday with friends in attendance.

Incarceration allowed Hitler time to think and design a grand strategy to elevate him to eventually become the supreme leader of the German nation. It was an achievement that would prove to have catastrophic consequences for the world. The solitude of a spacious cell was conducive to define and refine his ideology and commit it to writing. Sunlight streamed through a large window from which he could gaze upon the street below and illuminate his writing at a table where he typed on his portable typewriter. He was provided with newspapers, granted walks outside the building, and received visitors who brought him gifts, including food, and the benefit of conversation and a lifeline to the world beyond his cell. The prison management and guards were sympathetic to his nationalist fervor.

On December 20, 1924, Hitler was released four years earlier than his sentence, due to good behavior. His nine months of confinement had given him time to reflect, to plot his future, and to write. Many believe this critical period of his life was transformational.

The cell was a petri dish, an incubator for evil.

Sold for 12 marks, or the equivalent of $3, *Mein Kampf* was priced at nearly double the price of most books sold in Germany. The publishing company's contention that 23,000 copies were sold in its first year and subsequent sales figures were met by some with skepticism. Records seized by the Allied Forces after WWII included documents that revealed that book sales fell short of that figure, and that in fact 9,473 copies were sold the first year. Sales then decreased for a time. With Hitler's dramatic ascension to the highest echelon of power in the German government, the uptick in sales was substantial. Hitler's power and purchases of *Mein Kampf* accelerated in tandem. By 1932, sales of *Mein Kampf* spiked to 90,351 and the royalties became Hitler's main source of income.[13]

---

[13] William Shirer, *The Rise and Fall of the Third Reich: A History of Nazi Germany*, Simon and Shuster, New York, 1960, pp. 80-81. Shirer was a journalist and war correspondent, and originally a foreign correspondent for *United Press International* (UPI). *The International News Service*, that had employed Cranston, later merged with UPI.

1933

Mein Kampf is a bestseller.
Hitler subsequently
becomes a millionaire.

Party members began buying *Mein Kampf* in droves. Different book covers were specifically designed for certain groups of the German populace. There was a version with a blue cover for German soldiers, and others were produced for students upon graduation. A special edition was issued as gifts to all German newlyweds. Hitler adamantly opposed Aryan inter–marriage with other races, believing that such unions would dilute the Aryan race. He promulgated the belief that Aryans should rule over all other races and peoples whom he believed to be inferior, and even subhuman. The Cranston edition highlighted a passage in Chapter X of *Mein Kampf* setting it off in a box that stated:

> *"Marriage must not be thought of as an end in itself, for it has one great design: propagation and preservation of the race. This is its sole meaning."*

When Hitler became Chancellor in 1933, *Mein Kampf* sales skyrocketed to one million copies. His royalties increased from 10 to 15 percent. By 1940, six million copies of *Mein Kampf* had been sold in Germany, ranking second only to the sales of the Bible.[14] *Mein Kampf* became so influential that some

---

[14] *Ibid.*, p.81.

called it the Nazi Bible. The juxtaposition of these books on the bestseller list, and their diametrically opposite message, is irony personified. Hitler inspired a sizable population of Germany to follow him with a devotion that was almost religious in its fervor. The former nearly destitute struggling artist had become a millionaire.

In the world–wide bestselling classic, *The Rise and Fall of the Third Reich, A History of Nazi Germany,* William Shirer wrote, "Not every German who bought a copy of *Mein Kampf* necessarily read it. I have heard many a Nazi stalwart complain that it was hard going and not a few admit—in private—that they were never able to get through to the end of its 782 turgid pages. But it might be argued that had more non–Nazi Germans read it before 1933 and had the foreign statesmen of the world perused it carefully while there still was time, both Germany and the world might have been saved from catastrophe. For whatever other accusations can be made against Adolf Hitler, no one can accuse him of not putting down in writing exactly the kind of Germany he intended to make if he ever came to power and the kind of world he meant to create by armed German conquest. The blueprint of the Third Reich and, what is more, of the barbaric New Order which Hitler inflicted on conquered Europe in the triumphant years between 1939 and 1945 is set down in all its appalling crudity at great length and detail between the covers of this revealing book."[15]

---

[15] *Ibid.*

Part III

Cranston In Europe

Launched into the world after graduating from Stanford in June 1936, Cranston was eager to become a journalist overseas. He began doing unpaid odd jobs in London at the headquarters of the Hearst wire service, International News Service (INS). (In 1958, INS merged with United Press which was renamed United Press International.) His diligence paid off and he was hired as foreign correspondent at a salary of $5 a day. Cranston was elated. He wrote home, "It's the most fascinating work on earth." Later, Cranston was promoted to assistant manager of INS in Rome where he became more proficient in Italian. There, he witnessed the rise of Mussolini.

Cranston saw Hitler twice in person, both times in Munich. The first was during the summer of 1934 when he was a sophomore and happened to be in the same room with Hitler. The second occasion was when he saw Hitler on a street. He had watched on the sidelines at one of Hitler's speeches and the public's reaction. Hitler could talk for long stretches of time, yet the attention of his audience did not wane or wander at any point. Hitler's energetic speaking style used hand gestures punctuating key points. He exuded supreme confidence. The nationalism that he stoked and the almost religious devotion he commanded continued to expand. Cranston was intrigued by this phenomenon named Adolf Hitler. He explored the cities he visited and spent time with Germans to learn from them, asking questions about their views of Hitler—probing and trying to get to the core of Hitler's mesmerizing appeal. Young, but astute and discerning, Cranston grew increasingly unsettled by what he had witnessed and heard in Hitler's Nazi Germany.

Even before his foreign correspondent work reporting for INS, Cranston had witnessed the mistreatment of Jews in Germany on his earlier visits. Spending more time in Europe and travels to Germany, he saw the rise of persecution of Jews up close. Some anti–Semitic actions were overt and blatant. Signs of "Jews Not Welcome" hanging outside establishments were common. Jews were barred from German citizenship. Marriage between Jews and Aryans was forbidden. During the 1936 Berlin Summer Olympics, such publicly displayed anti–Semitic signs were removed temporarily in an effort to avoid controversy and to impress the British and American visitors to the German nation and society.

Shortly after arriving in the London INS office, Cranston was assigned to file reports on the 1936 Summer Olympics through telegrams received from Berlin. This was a natural assignment for him—given his twin talents as sprinter and journalist. Ironically, Adolf Hitler's plan was to use the Berlin Games as a high–profile demonstration to affirm his conviction and ideology of Aryan racial superiority.

Instead, a non–Aryan, African–American named Jesse Owens won four gold medals in the 100–meter, 200–meter, the 400–meter relay, and long jump. Triumphant after the Berlin Olympics, the U.S team traveled to London to compete in a track meet at the Crystal Palace. Cranston covered the event. Owens and Cranston became easy companions as they explored London together. Owens confided to Cranston that he had plans for a political career and leveraging his fame to improve black–white race relations. Although Cranston filed reports based on his interviews with Owens, they did not appear under his name. Instead, parts were used in other articles.[16]

Ralph Metcalfe, another African–American Olympic medalist on the team with Owens, led the American 400–meter relay team to a world record. Like Cranston, Metcalfe would eventually be drawn to politics. Decades later, both won elections to Congress: Metcalfe (D–IL, 1971–1978) to the House of Representatives, and Cranston (D–CA, 1969–1993) to the Senate. They had crossed the Atlantic then became legislators in their respective chambers in the U.S. Capitol.

The Berlin Games made television history by being the first Olympics that was broadcast. The new technology enabled the number of people who watched the games to increase exponentially. Relatively few people owned television sets, but approximately 150,000 people in Berlin watched the Games in public viewing rooms. The footage of this Olympics was preserved for all time—capturing the fallacy of Hitler's Aryan supremacy theories in perpetuity. News coverage also showed Hitler's charismatic effect on German citizens on a grand scale.

---

[16] Fowle, p. 25, and Robinson, p. 89.

Hitler's popularity continued to rise. To aid his ascent to power, he exploited the unhealed wounds from Germany's defeat in WWI and the punitive terms of the Treaty of Versailles: the redrawing of boundaries and the imposition of harsh reparations. Stoking embers, he poked at the open and festering wound. His call to German nationalism and return to its former status in the world resonated with disaffected Germans. His passionate speeches held people enthralled. In the Foreword to *Mein Kampf*, Hitler stated, "I know that people are won more by the spoken than by the written word, that every great world movement depends upon great speakers, not upon great writers."

Cranston witnessed the emerging power shifts in Europe, including the rise of Mussolini. For four months, he reported firsthand the Fascist occupation of Ethiopia where he travelled extensively and heard shooting every night. This was a time of discovery and learning about the world and about himself. It was the adventurous and glamorous life he had dreamed about, but he learned that there was another side to the adrenaline rush and excitement of reporting on breaking news. Cranston saw the darker side, the brutal ravages of war and human suffering up close. These harrowing images and experiences affected him deeply and influenced him for the rest of his life.

He had also reported from London at the time of the Munich Agreement, and was disturbed by Neville Chamberlain's appeasement. Cranston also grew concerned about the persistent voices of American isolationism that left many Americans unaware or uncaring about world events an ocean away, events that would eventually affect them.

His own eyes and a gut feeling that the gathering storm clouds of war were on the horizon brought Cranston to the realization that he needed to do more than observe and report. He believed in journalism, not only as an honorable profession, but for its value to inform and educate the public. At the same time, he came to see its limitations without tangible impact or results as quickly as he would like.

He wanted to make things happen, to be in the thick of it—not on the sidelines watching. Cranston resolved to make a difference, and that meant seeking ways to be active, not reactive, to unfolding events that were harbingers of terrible things to come. He determined to be involved in American politics or government in some way.

It was time to come home.

"The only thing necessary for the triumph of evil is for good men to do nothing."

Edmund Burke

"Sunlight is said to be
the best of disinfectants."

Louis Brandeis, December 20, 1913
Later Associate Justice,
U.S Supreme Court of the United States,
1916–1939

Part IV

Exposing Hitler In His Own Words

What did Americans really know about Adolf Hitler, Nazi Germany, and the possibility of another European war?

In the mid–to late 1930s, there was no consensus on whether the United States should fight in another European conflict if tensions deteriorate into war. The motivation behind the stance of both isolationists and interventionists was not simple. A myriad of concerns and national issues such as the Depression and economic recovery contributed to an America–first mentality tempered by aversion to foreign entanglements and memories of the high cost of WWI in both lives and treasure. Some felt war was inevitable, that America would eventually be drawn in again into the European arena. Hitler's anti–Semitism was not new but it gained more traction and attention with its increasingly blatant persecution of Jews. Among these were the 1935 Nuremberg Laws which officially barred Jews from German citizenship and institutionalized the legal definition of who was a Jew.

On November 9 and 10, 1938, German propaganda minister Joseph Goebbels orchestrated violence against Jews across the Reich. The assassination of a German embassy official in Paris by a Jewish teenager was used to ignite German anger against Jews. This pogrom was known as *Kristallnacht*, the Night of Broken Glass because there was so much broken glass from the attacks against Jewish shops and other establishments scattering the streets. Violence and looting were rampant. Over 250 synagogues, 7,000 Jewish businesses, cemeteries, schools, homes, and hospitals were attacked. Dozens of Jews were killed while German police and fire brigades did nothing to intervene or stop the rampage. Yet German Jews were blamed for the violence perpetrated against them, resulting in the arrest of 30,000 Jews who were sent to concentration camps where they subsequently died from the brutality. The government imposed a crushing $400 million (U.S. dollars) on the German

Jewish community. *Kristallnacht* and the ensuing laws made it legal to take Jewish property and livelihood that led to the mass emigration of Jews.

New Deal programs and the economy preoccupied President Franklin D. Roosevelt as he considered his options with Hitler and Mussolini's aggression in Europe and Japan's militarism in Asia. On November 5, 1940, Roosevelt won an unprecedented third term as President. During the campaign, he promised not to send American troops into foreign wars. He faced enormous responsibilities and challenges in and out of the public eye. Nicknamed "the Sphinx" for his extraordinary intellect and cunning, he was a master politician and statesman in complex relationships with his Cabinet, Congress, labor unions, business community, the press, the public, and foreign leaders.[17]

As Hitler's power continued to rise unabated, the debate between American interventionists and isolationists gained traction. Some favored intervention based on principles of aiding European allies and standing with democracies under German attack while others were convinced that America must first take care of its own people who were struggling to

---

[17]For an in−depth examination of Roosevelt's challenges, see Nicholas Wapshott, *The Sphinx: Franklin Roosevelt, The Isolationists, and the Road to World War II*, New York, 2015.

dig out of the impact of WWI and the Great Depression. Among isolationists in Congress against America entering a war were Senators William Borah (R–ID, who served on the Senate Committee on Foreign Relations), Burton Wheeler (D–MT), Gerald Nye (R–ND). Isolationists in the House included Representatives Hamilton Fish (R–NY), Dewey Short (R–MO), and Karl Mundt (R–SD).

Former President Herbert Hoover, President Roosevelt's immediate predecessor, was publicly vocal about his stance on the war and peace debate in August 1939, only a month before Germany invaded Poland. Hoover reminded the public in vivid detail the horrors of WWI in an article, "Shall We Send Our Youth to War?" He stated in part, "We were actually at the front in this war for only a few months, but it cost us the lives of 130,000 men. It has cost us 40 billions of dollars. A large segment of our people has already been impoverished for a quarter of a century. And the end is not yet. We may need to go to war again. But that war should be on this hemisphere alone and in defense of our firesides or our honor. For that alone should we pay the price."[18]

---

[18] Herbert Hoover, "Should We Send Our Youth to War?" *The American Magazine,* August, 1939. Condensed in *Readers Digest.*

The 1930s witnessed the media near–omnipotence of William Randolph Hearst's expanding empire. He controlled and owned the largest publishing conglomerate in the United States, including 28 newspapers, magazines, radio stations, and motion picture studios. The Hearst newspapers solicited and paid Hitler and Benito Mussolini for their columns. When Hitler demanded pay parity with Mussolini, Hitler was rejected because a Hearst editor deemed Hitler's writing and timeliness not up to standards to warrant an increase. Subsequently, in 1934, Hitler's chief henchman Hermann Goring succeeded him as the German expert for the Hearst papers. Hearst also owned INS which employed Cranston from 1936–1938.

Hearst favored nationalism and putting American interests first, but he was intrigued by fascism and met with Hitler in 1934. He later tried to portray the meeting as an opportunity to try to convince Hitler away from his anti–Jewish stance. A powerful influence in politics, Hearst exercised his considerable power of the press to oppose and criticize President

Roosevelt on the New Deal, and even linked the program to communism.[19]

Reporting on Germany by American and other newspapers was not always flattering to Hitler, but they were no match for Hitler's well–placed phalanx of propaganda during his ascendency. For nearly all of the 1930s, Hitler's carefully orchestrated propaganda machine was working overtime and proved effective. The November 1938 issue of the British magazine, *Home & Gardens*, and other publications produced fluff pieces on Hitler. He was portrayed as a country gentleman, a vegetarian, who enjoyed relaxing in his mountain chalet in the Bavarian Alps on breaks from his government duties. He neither smoked nor drank! Hitler was photographed smiling benevolently talking to local young children.

In addition to newspapers, Americans got their news from radio broadcasts, magazines, and newsreels shown in movie theaters. Radio journalism became the source of both news and entertainment.[20]

---

[19]David Nasaw, *The Chief, The Life of William Randolph Hearst*, (Boston, New York: Houghton Mifflin Co., 2000).

[20] Television was demonstrated at the World's Fair in 1939, and only introduced in Italy and Japan during that same year. As mentioned earlier, 150,000 people in Berlin watched the 1936 Olympics in public television viewing rooms because few owned

The 1930s also saw the emergence of columnists as part of the news culture.[21] The syndication of regular columns in the newspapers gave columnists a voice to their opinions across the nation. Many gained a following and a measure of influence.

Life magazine provided a selection of syndicated columnists' views on the war and peace debate.[22] For example, First Lady Eleanor Roosevelt, who had her own column (68 newspapers with over 4.4 million circulation) weighed in on the debate: "The newspapers these days are full of wars and rumors of wars, but I do not think the contention that this country is in need of a society to keep us out of war is

---

personal television sets. In America, widespread availability of television sets did not occur until the post–war years.

[21] The United States Holocaust Memorial Museum (USHMM) in Washington, D.C., has undertaken a citizen history research project to chronicle how US newspaper across the country reported on events of the Holocaust from 1933–1945. Topics for research include *Kristallnacht* and key moments during the refugee crisis in 1938–1939. Volunteers contribute to the project by searching newspapers from their local and state newspapers and uploading their findings to the History Unfolded website. The findings will help scholars and the general public learn more about American press coverage of the Holocaust. See https://newspapers.ushmm.org/ (accessed on Sept. 10, 2017) for more information.

[22] "The Nation's Columnists Debate on War and Peace," *Life,* April 24, 1939. Reprinted in *Reader's Digest,* June 1939, pp. 18–21.

well founded. Have we decided to hide behind neutrality? It is safe, perhaps, but I am not sure it is always right to be safe. Every time a nation which has known freedom loses it, other free nations lose something, too."

Hugh Johnson (76 newspapers with 5.3 million circulation) wrote "No matter who wins, the next world war will permanently destroy the democracy of every nation that gets into it. If we want to save democracy for the world we will keep out of European war."

Dorothy Thompson (196 newspapers with 7.5 million circulation) wrote in part, "...the world is in the most serious crisis in at least 400 years. It is perhaps the most serious crisis since the collapse of the Roman Empire...The Nazi–Fascist movement cannot be isolated except by resistance. We are already engaged in a struggle which will certainly result in war or in the defeat of this whole American way of life without war, unless we are willing to use right now the political and economic weapons which are in our hands."

Walter Lippmann (184 newspapers with 7.1 million circulation) wrote, "Senator Borah and his associates talk as if the issue before Congress were whether the United States will go into or stay out of the next war. That is not the issue. The issue is whether there is or is not going to be another world war. The question is whether the power and influence of this nation can be used now, before it is too late, to prevent war, to prevent our having to make the horrible choice which will confront us if war breaks out, the choice which will haunt us as long as it lasts. If there is another world war it will be fought on every continent and in every ocean. There is no guarantee against entanglement in a world war except diplomacy which prevents the war."

Walter Winchell (150 newspapers, 8.5 million circulation): "Once again Europe is rolling the loaded dice of destiny. And once again America is asked to play the role of international sucker. The time has come for us to pause and consider. If we must have an Unknown Soldier – let us not ask him to die for an unknown reason! And just what will be accomplished by dying in the mud? ...The future of American youth is on top of American soil–not underneath European dirt."

Alan Cranston returned to the United States just in time for Christmas in 1938. He moved into an apartment in New York City. While at Macy's department store in the city, his attention was riveted to a book display of *Mein Kampf.* Flipping through the book, Cranston became suspicious of this noticeably thinner and lighter version of the book he had read in Germany. He knew immediately that the translated copy was not the same original German *Mein Kampf.* He fished out the $3 (the equivalent of $53.16 in 2017 dollars) from his pocket and bought a copy.[23]

The book cradled in his large hands was an abridged English translation. Sanitized. This *Mein Kampf* version omitted Hitler's most nefarious tenets. The revelation propelled him to call his good friend, Hearst editor Amster Spiro, the seasoned former city editor of the *New York Journal.* Spiro had been helpful to Cranston when he was job–hunting soon after graduation by introducing him to potential employers in the journalistic world. For some time both Cranston and Spiro had been exploring innovative ways of publishing that would offer less expensive options to American readers. Now, with this jarring discovery, Cranston immediately turned to Spiro. Together they came to the same conclusion. Hitler posed an unacceptable existential danger to the world. This madman must be stopped. A strategy was devised to publish a shorter version translated from the original German *Mein Kampf.* A sense of real urgency spurred them to action.

---

[23] Constant dollar converted from Bureau of Labor Statistics, Department of Commerce, Consumer Price Index Inflation Calculator.

The race against Hitler was on.

Cranston and Spiro each brought their particular strengths to the mission. Cranston consulted various German editions of *Mein Kampf*, then translated, analyzed, and wrote a condensed English version with explanatory notes and commentary. His edition highlighted passages from the original *Mein Kampf* that revealed the full extent of Hitler's ideology of Aryan supremacy, his chilling anti–Semitic beliefs, and his hunger for power to dominate the world.

Spiro brought his entrepreneurial and publishing acumen to the endeavor to form Noram Publishing Company, which subsequently was incorporated on March 31, 1939. He moved quickly to contract services for printing and distribution with Caslon Publication Service, Inc., and Interborough News Company. The completed Cranston edition was a condensed version of the original book from about 270,000 to a more digestible 70,000 words contained in 32 newspaper-sized pages. The title—*Adolf Hitler's Own Book Mein Kampf (My Battle)*—was emblazoned on the cover of the publication in tabloid style. The cover also boldly stated that this version provided "Critical Comments and Explanatory Notes" and "Complete in this Issue….Unpublished Nazi Propaganda Maps Exposing Hitler's 10 Year Plan for Conquest of Europe.".

The Cranston–translated edition was sold for 10 cents a copy. At that time, the *New York Times* daily was 3 cents a copy in the city, and 4 cents elsewhere. A copy of *Reader's Digest* was priced at 25 cents. The Cranston edition would not only expose Hitler by using Hitler's own words against him but its low price could deprive Hitler his share of the 40 cents' royalty he had been receiving from the $3 copy.

In cartoon style, splashes of bold red color accented the book cover. It depicted Hitler hovering over a map of Europe—each hand holding Italy and Great Britain as if they were puzzle pieces to fit into his master plan. For purposes of economy and readability, Cranston eliminated Hitler's labored repetitive prose and rambling rants, yet retained the salient passages and the essence of the true meaning and intent of Hitler's blueprint. The format included boxes to set off Hitler's disturbing thoughts and motives. Cranston wrote headings to draw attention to the most alarming passages, then offered his own commentary and annotation.

Working at breakneck speed over eight days, Cranston wrote and hired a battery of secretaries to produce the translation. One of the secretaries, a young woman, did not understand Cranston's intent. As she began typing his early drafts, she grew suspicious of

Cranston. In her eyes, he appeared a man obsessed, working tirelessly, speaking rapidly with words that echoed some of Hitler's very words. Not knowing what to make of this tall lanky Cranston fellow, she reported her concerns to the Anti–Defamation League (ADL).

Soon after receiving her call, Benjamin Epstein of the ADL visited Cranston in his apartment. He discussed with Cranston what he had learned from the secretary. In short order, Cranston cleared up the misunderstanding by taking Epstein into his confidence about his purpose. Much relieved and interested, Epstein (who had lived in Berlin as a student a few years earlier) offered his assistance. Cranston's personal files show that Epstein introduced Cranston and Spiro to people who were in a position to help expand distribution of the Cranston edition in San Francisco, Los Angeles, and other metropolitan Western cities.[24]

---

[24] Benjamin Epstein letter to Richard Gutstadt dated April 27, 1939, Alan Cranston Papers, Bancroft Library, University of California at Berkeley. At the time, Gutstadt was the national Director of the Anti–Defamation League (ADL) since 1931. In the 1930s, he worked and lectured throughout the country, and organized opposition to the growing Fascist movement in the U.S. Later, Epstein became his successor as the ADL national director (1947–1978).

April 10, 1939

Alan Cranston's translated, condensed, and annotated version of *Mein Kampf* hits the newsstands.

The Cranston edition's *Publisher's Foreword*, stated, "Rival publishers have recently put two unabridged unexpurgated editions on the American market. They are bestsellers. People throughout the United States must wait months for their turn to obtain Mein Kampf from lending libraries. But Mein Kampf should be read today!"

The Cranston edition was designed to be more accessible, affordable, and readable in order to spread the word widely and quickly, with commentary to alert the public about Hitler. It was published, as Cranston described in his own words, as a "tabloid" on low−cost paper to reduce printing costs, with an attention−getting "lurid" cover showing Hitler trying to carve up Europe. Cranston also referred to the edition as similar to the popular *Reader's Digest* because of its condensed format.

Operating on a startlingly short deadline and limited budget, Cranston and Spiro contacted as many news dealers as they could to make the case for the condensed version and to maximize distribution. A one−page flyer appealed to news dealers to do "your bit to **STOP HITLER!"** In an urgent description of his edition, Cranston's bold language convinced them to sell his edition at their newsstands. The flyer stated:

IT IS IMPORTANT FOR EVERY AMERICAN, REGARDLESS OF RACE, NATIONALITY OR CREED TO READ THIS BOOK. AND KNOW WHAT THIS MAN PROPOSES, SO THEY CAN GUARD AGAINST HIM.

News dealers were urged to display an accompanying flyer that would promote vigorously the sale of "HITLER's own book—MEIN KAMPF in the new Noram Publishing Company TABLOID EDITION at 10 cents..." [25]

The Cranston edition hit the newsstands on or about April 10, 1939. In 10 days, half a million copies were sold. Their success attracted positive attention, but also from unwanted, nefarious elements. Newsstands selling the Cranston edition, including those in St. Louis, New York, and other cities, were attacked. Some were assailed with stink bombs, and others were overturned. Cranston attributed these acts to Hitler's minions or other Nazi sympathizers. Intimidation was not a word in the Cranston lexicon. If anything, the attack proved to Cranston and Spiro that they were precisely on the right track and striking the right chord. Their resolve remained steadfast and

---

[25] Alan Cranston Papers, Bancroft Library, University of California Berkeley.

they were not diverted from their mission. Sales of the Cranston edition continued.

In hindsight, it is surprising that Hitler's camp did not take more drastic measures to further obstruct or stop the Cranston version. There is no indication that any physical harm came to Noram Publishing Company's officers or that any direct threats were made against them other than the attacks on the newsstands. One might speculate that any serious violence—if ever considered—would have been counterproductive and proved the very point that Hitler and his henchmen were dangerous. History tells us that at the time, Hitler was occupied with implementing the next steps in his grand plan of conquest. Hitler's army had already invaded and occupied Czechoslovakia on March 15, 1939. Poland was next. The Nazi war machine invaded Poland on September 1, 1939, which marked the beginning of World War II.

On April 26, 1939, the Houghton Mifflin Company[26] filed a lawsuit in the Southern District Court of New York against Noram Publishing

---

[26] Based in Boston, Massachusetts, Houghton Mifflin Company is a well-established publishing house.

Company for infringing the copyright laws of the United States.

On July 14, 1939, U.S. District Judge Edward Conger ordered a preliminary injunction against the Cranston edition. Judge Conger enjoined Noram Publishing Company, Inc., Caslon Publication Service Inc., Interborough News Company, and the officers of Noram Publishing from "directly or indirectly publishing, printing, reprinting, translating, copying, distributing, vending or offering for sale a certain copyrighted work entitled 'Mein Kampf' by Adolf Hitler, or part of said work, and from in anywise infringing the rights on said work" pending resolution of the lawsuit.

However, Cranston had accomplished what he had set out to do – he had exposed Hitler.

Americans who were waitlisted for weeks or months at their local lending library to read *Mein Kampf* now could forego the wait and purchase the shorter version for a mere dime rather than pay 30 times more for Hitler's book. A spotlight shone on Hitler's own words and more Americans were informed about Hitler's true intent.

The Cranston edition's *Publisher's Foreword*:

"*This book, MEIN KAMPF, written in 1925 by an obscure German political prisoner, is a startling, almost miraculous prophesy, of present day as it is being made by Adolf Hitler.*

The reader of Mein Kampf is always amazed at the completeness with which Hitler is carrying out his fantastic aims. It seems incredible that after having set down in writing such brutal, coldly–calculated plans. Hitler is being allowed by his fellow Germans—and by the rest of the world—even to attempt to execute them.

If Hitler's plans as stated in Mein Kampf are carried out—if he is not stopped—they mean inevitable war, bloodshed, and the destruction of civilization as we know it.

The reader of his strange book is never able to understand how Hitler can sneer at the masses, call them dull, stupid, moronic –and still captures them.

But—usually the individual never quite considers himself a member of the great menace. It is always his near neighbor who is dull, stupid!

Also—wild, rambling Mein Kampf never attracted much attention until Hitler was powerful enough actually to execute the chilling plans outlined in his book.

Finally—the German edition of Mein Kampf— which has made Hitler a millionaire through laws making it compulsory that it be read in the Nazi state and that it be presented to all newly wedded couples—was carefully expurgated. So was the British edition—and the French edition. Each country was offered only a specially–prepared edition. None were allowed to know the true and full measure of Mein Kampf.

The book first appeared in America in an abridged carefully expurgated edition to which were omitted certain basic principles and ambitions which it behooved Hitler to conceal from American eyes.

Millions of copies of Mein Kampf have now been bought and read all over the world, for it has become the most vital and significant political tract of our time. Rival publishers have recently put two unabridged unexpurgated editions on the American market. They are bestsellers. People throughout the United States must wait months for their turn to obtain Mein Kampf from lending libraries.

But Mein Kampf should be read today!

Every living American should know–immediately–exactly what it was that Hitler said back in 1925—for now words are finding expression in acts of aggression, persecution, tyranny!

It is impossible to understand the ever-changing world of today without knowing the most important ideas and plans Hitler wrote down in Mein Kampf. Yet in the complete edition of Mein Kampf it is a trying, tiresome task to rescue what is coherent thought from the midst of Hitler's torrent of 270,000 words.

This edition of Mein Kampf contains every important point, every important idea Hitler presented, every important sentence he wrote. Hitler's inconsistencies, self-contradictions, extremities, even his erratic language–all these are retained here.

But we have eliminated his long-winded digressions, and cut out much of the endless repetition–repetition which he himself explains is necessary in order indelibly to impress an idea upon the mind of everyone exposed to his propaganda.

Sometimes we have expressed in a single sentence a thought which Hitler required two or three pages to present. We have slashed Hitler's 270,000 words to 70,000. But nothing important is omitted!

All important portions of the text, expurgated in the original American-edition, are presented here. The reader of our edition will know exactly what Hitler said in Mein Kampf. He will have gained an indispensable background without which it is impossible even to attempt to understand the present world. He will perhaps see a bit more clearly the role he, as an individual, must play in this Hitler threatened age.

We have criticized, commented upon, and explained the text wherever it was considered necessary.

APRIL 26, 1939

Hitler's American publisher
sues Cranston's publisher for
copyright infringement.

Part V

Hitler's Publisher Sues
For Copyright Infringement

Houghton Mifflin Company had entered into an agreement on July 29, 1933, with Franz Eher Nachf. G.m.b.H. Munchen, which assigned existing copyrights of *Mein Kampf* and the exclusive right to publish and sell Hitler's *Mein Kampf* in the United States.

Houghton Mifflin subsequently published the abridged edition of *Mein Kampf.* The Cranston edition's Foreword notes that Houghton Mifflin and the New York publishing house Reynal & Hitchcock entered into an agreement in the weeks near the end of 1938 to publish and sell an unabridged edition of *Mein*

Kampf. Since March 1, 1939, this unabridged version had had been published and sold in accordance with their agreement.[27]

At the time of the *Houghton Mifflin Publishing v. Noram Publishing Co.* (28 F. Supp. 676) lawsuit, Houghton Mifflin was involved in another copyright infringement case, *Houghton Mifflin Publishing v. Stackpole Sons, Inc.* (104 F.2d 306). Stackpole also sought to publish a version of *Mein Kampf.* Houghton Mifflin eventually won the lawsuit.

The Cranston–translated edition made its debut in early April. Case files, including statements by the president of Houghton Mifflin, indicate that it was first sold by newsstands in New York on or about April 10, 1939.[28]

The most expedient way to expose Hitler's full ideology and plans in the abridged *Mein Kampf,* was to form a new publishing company. Thus, Spiro

---

[27] Information presented is gleaned from official court documents from Civil Case Files, 1938–1992, Records of the District Court of the United States, U.S. District Court for the Southern District of New York, National Archives.

[28] Although Cranston wrote and annotated his condensed edition in a compressed eight days, editing, formation of Noram Publishing Company, finding and contracting printers, distributors, as well as making deals with newsstands to carry the edition would have taken weeks prior to the actual printing and delivery to newsstands.

established Noram Publishing Company primarily to publish the Cranston edition.

Houghton Mifflin submitted documents to the court stating that it had contacted Noram to demand that it stop printing, publishing, distributing, and selling the Noram–published edition of *Mein Kampf.* Noram refused.

On April 26, 1939, Houghton Mifflin filed a complaint against Noram Publishing Company, Caslon Publication Service, Inc., Interborough News Company. A copyright infringement lawsuit was filed in the Southern District U.S Court of New York.[29] In *Houghton Mifflin Company v Noram Publishing Company,* Houghton Mifflin contended that the Noram edition competed with the Reynal & Hitchcock version and would diminish the value of its edition resulting in damages and loss of revenue to Houghton Mifflin.

The law firm of Hines, Rearick, Dorr & Hammond represented Houghton Mifflin.

Hoguet, Neary & Campbell, Esq. represented the defendants, Noram Publishing Company, Inc., Caslon Publication Service, Inc. and Interborough News

---

[29] 28 F. Supp. 676 (S.D.N.Y. 1939).

Company. The judge cited the Cranston–translated edition's *Publisher's Foreword* as sufficient evidence on which to base his ruling. In issuing the preliminary injunction, Judge Conger wrote, in part:

> *"I am satisfied that a temporary injunction should issue. I am not unmindful of the cases cited in defendant's brief, that the court should be chary about issuing a temporary injunction; that, in effect, it amounts to an adjudication before trial and that in many cases, irreparable harm may come to a defendant, with no appreciable benefit to a plaintiff by such injunction. However, it seems to me in this case, all of the facts warrant an injunction. I am satisfied that the issuance and sale of defendant's edition is real competition to plaintiff's copyrighted book.*

> *...It appears to me that the defendant, Noram Publishing Co., knowing, or at least suspecting, the claimed copyright of the plaintiff to the book "Mein Kampf," attempted to take advantage of the public interest in Hitler and devised this form of pamphlet or edition, to profit by the desire of the public to read about Hitler."*

Noram's attorneys based their defense against the copyright infringement suit on technicalities. They argued that Hitler's *Mein Kampf* was in the public domain because Hitler was a stateless person when he wrote *Mein Kampf* on two points. First, Hitler was no longer an Austrian citizen when he served in the German army during WWI and that he did not become a German citizen until 1932. Second, Hitler's copyright on *Mein Kampf* was registered in Austria and since Hitler's German army had subsumed Austria into the German state, the copyright no longer existed.

The wheels of the judicial system sometimes turn slowly. The case proceeded in court. Interrogatories ordered, depositions taken, and more information requested and provided. The months stretched on as each side pressed its case. 1939 became 1940, then early 1941.

Meanwhile, the wheels of the ferocious German tanks advanced and rolled through Europe leaving atrocities, death, and destruction in their wake. Under Hitler, concentration camps had been established in the 1930s, but in June 1940, what was to become the largest and most infamous camp was established: Auschwitz. It would become a symbol of inhumanity, terror, and the Holocaust. Hitler's plans became horrific reality.

January 23, 1941

The American court makes its ruling on copyright infringement.

Kim Cranston holds his father Alan's 1939 condensed edition of Mein Kampf in Alan Cranston's personal library. Photo taken by Alan's beloved grand daughter Evan in 2017.

Part VI

Court Decision

In the period between the court's preliminary injunction against Noram Publishing on July 14, 1939, and the court's final ruling on January 23, 1941, Hitler's army began executing his plan to conquer most of Europe. On September 1, 1939, the Germany army invaded Poland, the catalyst for Britain, France, Australia, and New Zealand to declare war on Germany two days later. Two days after the outbreak of war, the United States proclaimed its neutrality. After the fall of Poland and several months' pause in warfare (Sitzkrieg) until April 9, 1940, Germany's offensive resumed with its invasion of Denmark and Norway. Facing the formidable well–trained, well–prepared

German military, European countries then fell like dominos with Germany's May 10 invasion of France, Belgium, Luxembourg, and the Netherlands. Later the same month, Holland and Belgium surrendered to Germany followed by Norway's surrender in June. Germany also invaded Romania and Yugoslavia that year.

Italy declared war on Britain and France in June 1940. Germany began air raids on London and declared a blockade of the British Isles. As America's allies came under attack, Germany, Italy and Japan signed a mutual defense treaty, the Tripartite Pact, on September 27, 1940. The three nations together came to be known as the Axis Powers.

As Hitler ignited a conflagration across Europe, the American court made its ruling. On January 23, 1941, nearly two years after Houghton Mifflin filed its lawsuit, U.S. District Judge Murray Hulbert presided over the consent judgment on *Houghton Mifflin Company v. Noram Publishing Company.* The judgment was a permanent injunction against Noram. The court ordered the impoundment and destruction of all remaining copies of the Cranston–translated–Noram–published edition of *Mein Kampf.* Payment of damages for Houghton Mifflin Company was ordered, adjudged, and decreed. Amster Spiro, who was primarily responsible for Noram's establishment and operations to publish Cranston's condensed edition, was fined in the amount of $1,000. Months prior to the final ruling, Noram Publishing's office in New York City had closed and all operations had ceased.[30]

By the beginning of 1941, Hitler's plan to spread the Third Reich across the continent was well underway.

In January 1941, there was still no consensus in America on Hitler and Nazi Germany. Some were isolationists, including pacifists, who did not want another foreign war. WWI was still a not too distant memory for many. Others were unconvinced that Hitler needed to be stopped, or that it was America's responsibility to stop him. Germany's aggression continued with the invasion of Russia in June 1941.

On December 7, 1941, the Japanese launched a surprise attack on the U.S. naval base in Pearl Harbor near Honolulu. The ferocious strike was devastating—in two hours, the attack killed over 2,000 American soldiers and sailors and wounded hundreds more, and destroyed 20 naval ships; 8 battleships and

---

[30] After WWII, Houghton Mifflin Company paid its largest advance to Winston Churchill for his six–volume account of World War II (for which Churchill won the Nobel Prize in Literature), and published books by General George Patton.

300 airplanes. Isolationism was no longer an option. President Roosevelt called December 7 "a date which will live in infamy." The next day, the United States and Britain declared war on Japan.

On December 11, 1941, Germany and Italy declared war against the United States. Congress acted swiftly to declare war with only one lone vote cast against war with Germany. Lifelong pacifist Representative Jeannette Rankin (R–MT) –the first woman to be elected to Congress–was the only Member of Congress to vote against U.S. entering both World War I and World War II.

In January 1941, Cranston had been working for the Common Council for American Unity[31] in New York City for almost a year. The Council published a quarterly literary magazine, *Common Ground*, which highlighted the contributions of different ethnic, religious, and national groups to American culture. As the Council's Washington representative, his responsibilities were to help immigrants of all ethnic backgrounds acclimate to life in America, and to help

---

[31] *Common Ground* was funded by the Carnegie Corporation of New York. The editorial board included Pearl Buck and Langston Hughes. First Lady Eleanor Roosevelt was a contributor.

Americans adjust to having immigrants from Germany, Italy, Poland, and other countries live among them.[32]

On the day of Noram's loss in court—January 23, 1941—several hundred miles to the south of the New York court, Charles Lindbergh, acclaimed national hero for his flight across the Atlantic, testified before the House Foreign Affairs Committee. He spoke against adopting the Lend–Lease bill that would provide U.S. military aid to foreign countries engaged in the war. Lindbergh had been a leader of isolationists who were against the U.S. entering the war. Congress passed the bill, and President Roosevelt signed the Lend–Lease Act into law on March 11, 1941. The law authorized transfer arms and other defense materials for which Congress appropriated money to "the government of any country whose defense the President deems vital to the defense of the United States."[33]

---

[32] Cranston worked with Eleanor Roosevelt against setting up relocation camps for Japanese Americans. Decades later, as Senator, he led legislative and other efforts to champion civil and human rights.

[33] Lindberg's considerable expertise and knowledge of European military strength and American air power influenced his opposition to policies leading up to WWII. After Pearl Harbor and the U.S entered the war, he volunteered to join the Air Force but was denied. Although he served as a civilian consultant in the testing of fighter aircraft in the Pacific. He never changed his stance against the U.S fighting the war. Lindbergh's leadership role against American war involvement is documented in Wayne S. Cole's *"Charles A.*

The act supported the British war effort until the U.S. entered the war. Eventually, in addition to Britain, other countries such as Brazil, China, the Soviet Union, and others received American armaments to fight WWII. Some opposed the bill fearing that it would provide the president unbridled power to carry out undeclared wars. American soldiers may not have put boots on the ground, but the Act could allow nearly everything short of it by providing moral and tangible material support to allies fighting an increasingly fierce war.

Until it was clear that the lawsuit was not going well, Noram initially had planned to publish future editions on other subjects. At the end of the Cranston edition was an advertisement for sale of an 8–volume set of "University Classics" for $1.29. In addition, Noram also advertised for exclusive news stories by writers on special correspondent assignments. Responses came rolling in. A brown file folder in Cranston's personal files contained letters to Noram pitching all manner of stories. In his own hand, Cranston labeled this folder:

Lindbergh and the Battle Against American Intervention in World War II."

'39 Mad Mail Mein Kampf.[34]

As a result of the judgment and the financial toll, Noram Publishing Company was unable to publish other works. It appears Noram and its officers made no profits from the Cranston edition due to its low selling price, and the expenses incurred for its printing and distribution negated any gains. Moreover, unsold copies that were printed, and presumably already paid for, were destroyed by court order.

As ordered by the court, Noram Publishing Company destroyed the remaining copies of Cranston–translated–Noram–published editions of *Mein Kampf.* How many of these copies survived over the decades is unknown. They subsequently became collectors' items.

The U.S. court had stopped Noram from further operations and distribution after 500,000 copies had been sold in 10 days. If the court had not ruled against Noram, how many more people in the United States might have read and heeded Alan Cranston's dire

---

[34] The author examined the file in November 2015 on a visit to Kim and Colette Cranston's home in Los Altos, CA. and toured Alan Cranston's personal library. The library is much as he left it upon his unexpected death on Dec. 31, 2000.

warning about Hitler? Would the Cranston edition have ignited a more meaningful and impactful discussion about American involvement in countering Hitler in the months leading to and the early days of WWII? Would more time have made it possible to marshal the attention of the public, the press, government officials, legislators, and other decision makers? Would his message have extended and resonated beyond America's borders? Would his actions have put Hitler on trial in the court of world opinion?

We will never know.

Epilogue

On April 30, 1945, Adolf Hitler committed suicide. Escaping justice, he was never brought to trial for his crimes against humanity. He wanted to conquer the world and ended as master of an underground bunker.

Alan Cranston went on to raise a family and lead a full life far beyond the adventures he imagined as a boy. He became a journalist, author, businessman, California State Comptroller, and U.S. Senator. Over the years, he mentored generations of young people who chose public service inspired by his example, and developed leaders who followed in his footsteps to serve in the Senate and House or other elective office, and as Cabinet secretaries.

After Pearl Harbor, he was hired to set up the Foreign Language Division at the Office of Facts and Figures (OFF), under Librarian of Congress Archibald MacLeish, an advisor to President Roosevelt. OFF was later folded into the Office of War Information, where foreign languages were used to communicate with foreign speaking groups about how the draft worked, how price controls worked and other matters through the press and radio. His tasks included explaining to German Americans why the U.S. was fighting Hitler and to Italian Americans why the U.S. was fighting Mussolini. Cranston joined the Army and wrote for *Army Times* to explain to soldiers why America was fighting the war. During his Army days, he wrote *The Killing of the Peace* about the role of the Senate and isolationists in the failure of the League of Nations. His intent was to prevent any efforts (which did not materialize) to block the U.S. from joining the United Nations. The book ranked as one of the top 10 on the *New York Times* bestseller's list in 1945. Decades later, he wrote *The Sovereignty Revolution* about his philosophy about world government as an evolutionary process, and the need to think globally.

His dedication to public service began with the pursuit of the truth in exposing Hitler and the sanitized *Mein Kampf.* He never stopped seeking the truth and alerting Americans and the world to the existential threat to peace. The threat of nuclear war inspired him to run for the U.S. Senate, where he served for four terms, and as Democratic Whip for 14 years. In the Senate, he became known for his vote counting prowess, keen grasp of legislation, and relentless commitment to issues that included the environment, civil and human rights, and education.

He was pragmatic and reached across the aisle on many issues, including press freedom with Senator Barry Goldwater (R–AZ), and public housing with Senator Alfonse D'Amato (R–NY). While he was against the Vietnam War, he was a champion for Vietnam–era and all veterans. As Chairman of the Senate Veterans' Affairs Committee, he and Ranking Member Senator Alan Simpson (R–WY) worked in concert to secure veterans' rights and improve their benefits. The two Alans also switched roles as Chairman and Ranking Member on the Committee. As a member of the Senate Foreign Relations Committee, he played key roles on nuclear arms and foreign policy issues. He worked to reduce tensions with the Soviet Union, normalize relations with the People's Republic of China, and support peace efforts in the Middle East.

Alan Cranston worked to stop the nuclear arms race by crafting legislation, and forming coalitions. He led the fight for a nuclear arms freeze and shaped the debate on the Strategic Arms Limitation and START Treaties. While advocating arms reductions, it would not come at any price, he was adamant that any arms control agreement must be verifiable.

In 1983—38 years after Albert Einstein told him that nuclear weapons could wipe out the entire human race—the world's nuclear arsenal had the explosive power to destroy the equivalent of one million Hiroshimas.[35] The proliferation of nuclear weapons and the accelerated threat of nuclear war propelled him to seek the Democratic nomination for President in the 1984 elections running on two main issues: peace and jobs. Had he won, ending the nuclear arms race would have been the defining goal of a Cranston presidency. Although this was one race he did not win, he brought the nuclear threat issue before Americans across the country. Never one to look back, he looked forward and continued his leadership on arms control in the Senate and his warning about the real danger of nuclear war by design, accident, or miscalculation.

Alan Cranston, in his post–Senate career after 1992, renewed his determination to abolish nuclear weapons working tirelessly and relentlessly with grassroots organizations at the state and national levels and with world leaders to stop the arms race that could lead to WWIII. On matters of world peace and the

---

[35] Alan Cranston, "The Conference on the Long–Term Worldwide Biological Consequences of Nuclear War," *Congressional Record*, Nov. 17, 1983, pp. S33620–S33624. The conference was the result of a two–year study spearheaded by Carl Sagan and Paul Ehrlich on the catastrophic effects of a nuclear war, resulting in a "nuclear winter." This *Record* statement which included the summary of the study is part of the Carl Sagan Collection at the Library of Congress.

building of democratic institutions, his knowledge and counsel were widely sought after.

In 1999, he founded the Global Security Institute (GSI),[36] and with other national and international leaders and organizations, focused on world peace, security, and cooperation. GSI continues Alan Cranston's goal to advance the cause for nuclear non–proliferation and disarmament.

Alan Cranston's legacy is his life–long work for a nuclear–free, just, humane, and peaceful world.

---

[36] GSI's stated mission: "The Global Security Institute is dedicated to strengthening international cooperation and security based on the rule of law, with a particular focus on nuclear arms control, non–proliferation and disarmament. GSI was founded by Senator Alan Cranston whose insight that nuclear weapons are impractical, unacceptably risky, and unworthy of civilization continues to inspire GSI's efforts to contribute to a safer world. GSI has developed an exceptional team that includes former heads of state and government, distinguished diplomats, effective politicians, committed celebrities, religious leaders, Nobel Peace Laureates, disarmament and legal experts, and concerned citizens." For more information about GSI, see http://gsinstitute.org/ (accessed on Sept. 19, 2017).

Decades after the court ordered the destruction of all remaining copies of the Noram–published edition of *Mein Kampf,* Alan Cranston searched and found a private copy for sale. He paid $50 for a copy of his own work –a markup of 50,000 percent from the original newsstand price of 10 cents.

In 1980, R.E., wrote a book about her brother, *Cranston, the Senator from California*. Four years later, she updated her book. The distributor of this updated version was *Houghton Mifflin Company.*

December 31, 2015

Hitler's copyright for
Mein Kampf expired and its
ban in Germany was lifted.

February 2016

A new critical
annotated academic
version of *Mein Kampf*
is published and
becomes
a bestseller in
Germany.

January 2017

The critical annotated academic edition of Mein Kampf is still a bestseller.

Appendix

Tributes to Alan Cranston

Excerpts from Selected Tributes Honoring Alan Cranston Related to *Mein Kampf* Upon His Senate Retirement (1992)

"In addition to his important public service achievements, Senator Cranston has compiled a remarkable and diversified personal record. Foreign correspondent, playwright, author, businessman, artist, and athlete, his achievements are incomparable. No other Senator can boast of having been sued by Adolf Hitler, or of having set a world record in track and field."

Senator Edward Kennedy,
Tribute to Senator Alan Cranston,
Congressional Record, September 30, 1992

"...nearly six decades ago, a young American journalist from California published an unexpurgated version of Adolf Hitler's Mein Kampf — 'My Struggle' –revealing, as few had previously done, the true depth of the danger and the evil that Hitler embodied."

Senator Robert Byrd,
A Man of Vision Goes Home,
Congressional Record, October 8, 1992

"Alan Cranston's dedication to promoting world peace comes from a personal and varied experience with war. As a young journalist, he covered the rise of fascism in Europe. He translated and published an English version of Mein Kampf in America to warn the public of the threat of nazism."

Senator George Mitchell,
"Farewell to Senator Alan Cranston,"
Congressional Record, October 5, 1992

"Alan Cranston had returned to the United States after having served as a foreign correspondent for the International News Service in England, Germany, Italy, and Ethiopia. He read German. He had read 'Mein Kampf.' He happened on the English language

version in a New York bookstore. He was appalled by the thought that the American people were reading a wholly misleading version of a propaganda tract of immense power. With the energy and swiftness, he brought and still brings to the 100–yard dash, Alan Cranston sat down and produced a translation of the passages Hitler had left out of the expurgated edition. Half a million copies were sold at 10 cents apiece. A banner on the cover told readers, `This is the true version of `Mein Kampf,' and Hitler will not get a penny of the royalties.'"

Senator Daniel P. Moynihan,
Alan Cranston,
Congressional Record, October 8, 1992

"Senator Cranston is also a businessman, a writer/reporter, and an athlete. As a businessman, he made his mark in real estate and investment. As an athlete, Senator Cranston set the world record for 55–year olds in the100–yard dash in 1969. As a writer/reporter, Senator Cranston was notably sued, indirectly, by Adolf Hitler for writing a tabloid version of Hitler's book 'Mein Kampf.'"

Senator Strom Thurmond,
A Tribute to Senator Alan Cranston,
Congressional Record, October 3, 1992

"As a young journalist working in Germany in the 1930s he recognized the horrors unfolding under the regime of the 20th century's worst despot— Adolf Hitler. Alan Cranston knew what the world was up against. His tireless effort to have Hitler' autobiography published in this country resulted in the alarms being sounded to the rest of the world. Later on, Hitler's German publishers won a copyright lawsuit against Alan. But for Alan Cranston the loss in the courtroom was a victory— Hitler could no longer hide his vicious antisemitism and his hideous ambitions for the world."

Senator Howard Metzenbaum,
The Career of Senator Alan Cranston,
Congressional Record, October 8, 1992

"From his early days, Alan Cranston was a crusader against man's inhumanity to man and a vigorous advocate for the rule of law. In 1939, he translated a version of Hitler's 'Mein Kampf' to draw the American people's attention to the implications of the Nazi program."

Senator Claiborne Pell,
Alan Cranston: Crusader for Peace,
Congressional Record, October 2, 1992

"Alan Cranston's achievements prior to seeking public office are equally diverse and exceptional. An early pioneer in the struggle for world law, his book 'The Killing of the Peace' was rated one of the 10 best books of 1945 by the New York Times. And how many Senators have set a world record in track and field, and had the distinction of being sued by Adolf Hitler? As foreign correspondent, businessman, author, and artist, he has brought his vision and intelligence to each endeavor and career."

Senator Harris Wofford,
Tribute to Senator Alan Cranston,
Congressional Record, October 8, 1992

97

Lorraine H. Tong

Tributes at Alan Cranston Memorial, Excerpts about His Role to Expose Hitler and Mein Kampf

"While a correspondent he saw an English language version of "Mein Kampf," sanitized to hide the truth from Americans. He published his own version highlighting the worst of Hitler" and was sued by Hitler's publisher. While he lost the suit, half a million copies had already been distributed, helping to educate many about the true nature of nazism and Hitler."

Senator Barbara Boxer,
for herself and Senator Dianne Feinstein, in submitting Senate Resolution 12 – Relative to the Death of Alan Cranston, former United States Senator for the State of California, in honor of Alan Cranston, Congressional Record, January 22, 2001

"In 1939, Alan Cranston edited the first unexpurgated English translation of Adolf Hitler's "Mein Kampf" published in the United States in an effort to alert Americans to the dangers of the Third Reich. In fact, Senator Cranston had the very unique experience of being sued by Hitler for copyright violation for his work on this editing project and – in true Alan Cranston form – he wore

this as a badge of honor and demonstrated that he would stand up to anyone in pursuit of Democratic principles and ideals."

Senator Dianne Feinstein,
Tribute to Former California Senator Alan Cranston
Congressional Record, January 4, 2001

"...sued by Adolf Hitler for translating in next to no time a version of "Mein Kampf." Being a pre–World War II journalist and being smart enough to understand what was going to be advocated..."

Senator Maria Cantwell
Memorial Tribute to Alan Cranston
Hart Senate Office Building
February 6, 2001

"Well, I knew who Al was, I knew of his journalistic prowess, of his warning to his countrymen about Adolf Hitler, and the two versions of "Mein Kampf" one for domestic consumption and one for the naive and Alan was sending out the alert."

Senator Alan Simpson,
Tribute to Alan Cranston Memorial,
Congressional Record, April 24, 2001

Lorraine H. Tong

"As a young journalist, he reported on the rise of nazism in Germany, and was sued by Adolf Hitler for publishing an unsanitized version of "Mein Kampf" and revealing Hitler's true ambitions to the world."

Senator Harry Reid,
Relative to the Death of Alan Cranston,
Congressional Record, January 24, 2001

"As a reporter in Europe in 1936, he was among the first to recognize the evil of fascism for what it was. He chronicled the rise of Hitler and Mussolini. When he discovered that Hitler had authorized the export of a sanitized copy of "Mein Kampf" to America, he acquired a copy of the German text and had it translated accurately, with all its hideous lies restored. He sold copies for 10 cents – thus giving American some of its true glimpses into the real Hitler. A copyright infringement lawsuit brought by Hitler himself eventually forced Alan Cranston to stop selling copies of "Mein Kampf" in America. But nothing could ever stop him from speaking out against oppressors of freedom and human dignity."

Senator Tom Daschle,
Tribute to Senator Alan Cranston
Congressional Record, February 28, 2001

"Alan Cranston was above all else a man of peace. And he was a man of peace not as a matter of public policy, but as a matter of personal passion. Remember: This was a man who, in 1934, found himself in the same room as Adolf Hitler. Five years later, he wrote a critical English translation of Adolf Hitler's "Mein Kampf" in an effort to reveal the German leader's true plans. And he wore Hitler's ensuing lawsuit as a badge of honor, proud that he had stood up to try and warn the English-speaking world about the evils of nazism."

Senator John Kerry
Memorial Tribute to Alan Cranston
Hart Senate Office Building
February 6, 2001

"Alan's record of service spans the better part of the 20ᵗʰ century. He was a journalist who covered World War II, an author who warned Americans about the threat of Hitler, a leader of an organization that opposed discrimination against immigrants, long before that was fashionable."

Senator Tom Harkin,
Tribute to Alan Cranston
Congressional Record, February 26, 2001

"He fought against fascism and nazism, alerting people to the threat of Hitler, by exposing the virulent nature of Hitler's writing. This act of courage helped to show the world the importance of fighting this menace to freedom and democracy.

Representative Joe Baca
Tribute to Senator Alan Cranston
Congressional Record, February 6, 2001

"Alan Cranston began his crusade for peace early in his life as a journalist...he edited the first unaltered version of 'Mein Kampf' laying bare Hitler's racist beliefs, and inviting a lawsuit from the Fuehrer over copyright infringement."

Representative Tom Lantos,
Tribute to Senator Alan Cranston
Congressional Record, February 6, 2001
(Note: Representative Lantos was a Holocaust
survivor.)

107TH CONGRESS
1ST SESSION

S. RES. 12

Relative to the death of Alan Cranston, former United States Senator for
the State of California.

IN THE SENATE OF THE UNITED STATES

JANUARY 22, 2001

Mrs. BOXER (for herself and Mrs. FEINSTEIN) introduced the following
resolution; which was considered and agreed to

RESOLUTION

Relative to the death of Alan Cranston, former United States
Senator for the State of California.

Whereas Alan MacGregor Cranston had a long and distinguished career, beginning with service as a foreign correspondent and continuing with service in the United
States Office of War Information and in the United
States Army;

Whereas Alan Cranston was a leader in his State before com-
ing to the Congress, serving as State Controller of California for eight years;

Whereas Alan Cranston served the people of California with
distinction for 24 years in the United States Senate;

Whereas Senator Cranston was lifelong advocate for world
peace and the defense of democratic institutions;

Whereas Senator Cranston was an unwavering friend of the environment and California's remarkable natural resources;

Whereas Senator Cranston was a leader in the United States Senate in many areas, including the fields of affordable housing, mass transit, veterans affairs, civil rights and education; and

Whereas Senator Cranston left a lasting legacy in his post-Senate career through his efforts to curb the spread of nuclear weapons and to eliminate the scourage of nuclear weapons from the planet, efforts which continued until the day he died: Now, therefore, be it

1   *Resolved,* That the Senate has heard with profound
2 sorrow and deep regret the announcement of the death
3 of the Honorable Alan Cranston, former member of the
4 United States Senate.

5   *Resolved,* That the Secretary of the Senate commu-
6 nicate these resolutions to the House of Representatives
7 and transmit an enrolled copy thereof to the family of the
8 deceased.

9   *Resolved,* That when the Senate adjourns or recesses
10 today, it stand adjourned or recessed as a further mark
11 of respect to the memory of the Honorable Alan Cranston.

○

SRES 12 ATS

The author and Alan Cranston

Lorraine H. Tong with Alan Cranston's
translated and condensed edition of
Mein Kampf at the Library of Congress.

Photograph by David Rice.

About the Author

Lorraine H. Tong immigrated to America when she was six years old, and grew up in the Bay Area in California. She received her degree in International Relations, with a concentration in U.S.–China relations, from Stanford University. As Senator Alan Cranston's foreign policy legislative aide and advisor for eight years, her issue areas of responsibilities included U.S.–China normalization of relations, Taiwan Relations Act, U.S.-Soviet relations, the Middle East, human rights, and nuclear arms control. She also worked for Senator Jacob Javits on U.S.-China issues.

Her post–Senate career includes research and analytic work at the Library of Congress's Congressional Research Service on public policy, including appropriations, and Supreme Court issues.

For almost a decade, she was Professional Development Committee Chair of the Congressional Asian Pacific American Staff Association.

She and her family enjoy traveling and looking forward to new adventures.